CAI GUO-QIANG
INOPPORTUNE

MASS MoCA

CAI GUO-QIANG
INOPPORTUNE

MASS MoCA

Commissioned for Building 5
December 2004 – November 2005

Laura Steward Heon
Robert Pogue Harrison
Cai Guo-Qiang interviewed by Jennifer Ma

Foreword by Joseph Thompson

This publication accompanies the exhibition *Cai Guo-Qiang: Inopportune* organized by MASS MoCA and exhibited there in Building 5 from December 11, 2004 through November 2005.

MASS MoCA extends thanks to the artists, copyright holders, and rights holders of all the images in this book. Every effort has been made to contact copyright holders prior to publication.

Graphic design by Arjen Noordeman
Printed and bound in the U.S.A. by Kirkwood Printing, Wilmington, Massachusetts

MASS MoCA

1040 MASS MoCA Way

North Adams MA 01247

PH 413-664-4481

FAX 413-663-8548

www.massmoca.org

ISBN: 0-9764276-1-3

Photography:

Cai Guo-Qiang: Pg. 58/59, 63

Hiro Ihara: Pg. 10/11, 18, 47, 56 (bottom), 57, 61, 66, 69

Kevin Kennefick: Pg. 23 (bottom), 44/45, 46, 48, 50/51, 52, 53

Image Select / Art Resource: Pg. 23 (middle)

Jung Kim: 56 (top)

Museum of Fine Arts, Boston: Pg. 21, 23 (top)

Arjen Noordeman: Pg. 40, 41, 49

Dirk Pauwels: Pag. 67

Larry Smallwood: Pg. 42, 43

Scala / Art Resource: Pg. 25

CONTENTS

ACKNOWLEDGEMENTS

Major support for MASS MoCA's series of programs on contemporary Chinese art has been provided by the W.L.S. Spencer Foundation. Additional support has been provided by the Maxine and Stuart Frankel Foundation for Art, the Nimoy Foundation, Holly Angell Hardman and the Appelbaum-Kahn Foundation.

The complex task of planning, fabricating and installing Inopportune required the minds and hands of many, including:

From MASS MoCA: Dale Bradley, John Carli, H.L.Chesbro and Son, Laura Christensen, John Cox, Richard Criddle, Shawn Fogarty, Shea Kiley, Tom Merrill, Molly O'Rourke, Greg Scheckler, Larry Smallwood, Liza Statton, Chris Westhoff,

From Cai Studio: Jennifer Ma, Tatsumi Masatoshi, Charwei Tsai, Hong-kai Wang, Hong Hong Wu

Foreword

JOSEPH THOMPSON

Director

As Cai mentions in his interview, our staff and board had a complex reaction to his bold proposal: mesmerized by its scale, vivid imagery, and direct narrative power, at the same time we worried that its loaded subjects – terrorism, martyrdom, and the slippery concept of heroism – might be perceived as exploitative or simply inappropriate at this moment in history. While our commitment to the work – and to Cai – never wavered for an instant, we did have many serious discussions about it, drilling down on the meaning of the installation, and the significance of our alliance to it. Indeed, in the now six-year history of MASS MoCA, this was the only time that MASS MoCA's board of trustees engaged in a formal discussion about any single work of art. Personally, I was proud of our board for digging into the issues so intelligently (and passionately) and energized by the fact that the board's fundamental support was never in question, even from those trustees who asked the most probing questions.

This is more interesting than intramural. Art worth the name resists unilateral interpretation, evincing capacity for sustained visual and intellectual engagement: *Inopportune* met that test early on. Even before it took physical form, the installation turned out to be far more nuanced and subtle than a simple written description would ever portend. Secondly, the work became a dramatic example of the visual imperative of great art: As it turned out, our concerns that our public would be mortified by car bomb imagery and references to terrorism were utterly misplaced. The material presence of the work – its aspect in space and time, and the almost operatic sequencing of its imagery – evoked a wholly different set of responses than we imagined in the abstract. I don't quite know what it means that Americans today are more reflexively sensitive to images of animals under duress than to exploding cars, but this is unequivocally true. Our comment book is full of questions about Cai's gallery of arrow-shot tigers – *Inopportune Stage Two* – but to date, and after some 20,000 visitors (with 80,000 still to go) we've registered not one objection to the car bomb reference. In large part, this is because Cai's visual treatment of exploding cars is so stunningly beautiful, and in a way so indirect – the explosive moment is drawn out in time and space, awash in a spectacle of color and cascading light – that many simply do not associate the vehicular constellation with a terrorist act. Terrorism is not beautiful, so how can this be about that? The troubling answer, like some primal reflex to touch the wound, is at the core of the work.

In some ways, it's the artist's job to be opportunistic. It's certainly not his job to be appropriate: Parsing that falls to museums, and ultimately you, our public, who, we hope, will carry these images and their complex meanings with you to other theaters.

After *Inopportune* was installed, Cai explained that when he first proposed the four ideas which became the prime elements of this exhibition, he expected the museum to select perhaps one or two. When we opened a new gallery to accommodate the entire suite of works, Cai was too good a negotiator to act surprised: He never dropped his game face, saving his broad, charming smile and wonderful humor for leverage later in this great installation adventure.

But perhaps he was not surprised: Risk, generosity and ambition are at the very core of MASS MoCA's institutional DNA, though "institutional" is the wrong word, since in the end it's individual people who supply the creative octane, muscle, and craft that realized these vast productions. Our wonderful staff can, when it chooses, make almost anything happen by dint of will. Almost anything, I should say, but not quite everything, since the full achievement is impossible without deft support from a strong and effective Board, and from extraordinarily generous sponsors (in this case, most especially the W.L.S. Spencer and Nimoy Foundations). I know of no other institution better able to convert cash, sweat and professional skill into great art, and it's an exquisite pleasure when those resources combust with great artists like Cai Guo-Qiang.

Joseph Thompson
Director
In the year of the rooster

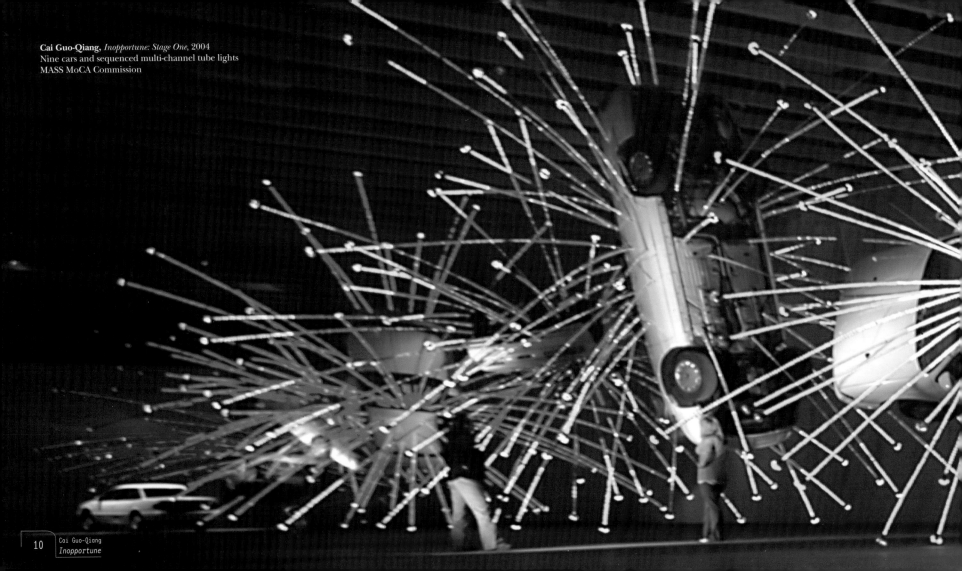

Cai Guo-Qiang, *Inopportune: Stage One,* 2004
Nine cars and sequenced multi-channel tube lights
MASS MoCA Commission

Cai Guo-Qiang
Inopportune

Inopportune

LAURA STEWARD HEON
Curator

On arrival at Cai Guo-Qiang's four-part installation *Inopportune* in MASS MoCA's Building 5, you descend into a very large, rectangular gallery from a raised landing. Dazzling, beautiful light suffuses the space, washing over every surface. Hundreds of long transparent rods pulsing with colored light thrust out from identical white cars that hang from the ceiling at vertiginous angles in a long arc down the center of the gallery. As you move further into the gallery, it becomes clear that there are nine cars, the first and last of which rest on the floor, which is lifted off the ground only slightly. Bright white lights race out of it to convey the detonation. From there, the position of the cars become more acrobatic, and the lights move through hot reds and oranges, pulsing quickly in cars three and four, to a full range of fantasy fireworks colors – pinks, greens, violets – bursting out in all directions from the middle cars. For the final two cars in the air, the lights slide into purple and indigo, which Cai describes as "dream colors," moving at an increasingly meditative pace. The deep indigo light tubes sweep out of the last airborne car like graceful wings, allowing the car to glide to a safe and gentle landing, quite different from its violent launch. The fact that the ninth car is not destroyed, but lands safely, unaltered, at the end, implies a closed and repeatable circuit. Time and space are conflated here; walking from one end of the gallery to the other, you move forward through time, and the pace of your walking controls the pace of the explosion, as if in a dream.

At the end of the long gallery containing this strange, spectacular, evocative installation, you enter a low, dark space with a video projected in a long horizontal format. Nine feet high and 35 feet long, the projection, titled *Illusion*, is big enough to envelope you. The scene is Times Square at night, pulsing with glittering neon, bustling traffic and traffic noise, and crowds of pedestrians, who, in the center of the projection, are nearly life-sized. Into this scene from the left floats a ghostly car like the ones in the preceding gallery. It follows the flow of traffic but appears "pasted" on top of the underlying action in Times Square, quite stylized and obviously fake. After a few seconds, sparks start to fly. Fireworks shoot out of the car, first just a few, then, as the car reaches the center of the projection, in giant bursts of color, light, and noise that obliterate the car. Gradually the explosions recede and the car disappears from the screen on the right. The people on the sidewalks and in the densely packed cars – and even a mounted policeman – are oblivious to what is happening right in front of them. Again as in a dream, you alone can see the explosion. In 90 short seconds, the car enters, explodes, and disappears, and then the video begins again, so that the car reenters continually. Passing behind the projection screen, which bisects the square room, you find the actual car that was used in filming the video, loaded with spent fireworks and badly charred, real evidence of your apparition.

Exiting this low, dark gallery of mesmerizing video into a stairway, you climb to a mezzanine gallery that affords an overview of the large gallery with the cars and lights. An expansive drawing – nearly 20 feet long and 12 feet high – hangs from the back wall of the gallery. The large circle that dominates the center of the untitled drawing was made by exploding gunpowder on the surface of the heavy paper. Silhouettes of nine cars are equally spaced around the circle, their ghostly outlines burned into the paper. Cai began making drawings with gun powder in 1984, a practice he has pursued intermittently since then and for which he is well known. The gunpowder drawing for *Inopportune*, as well as many other projects, serves as a poetic proposal, encapsulating the conceptual essence of the installation as a whole.

You pass back through all you have seen before to enter the final gallery, which, like the first, is long and narrow, though not so large. Here, you climb a few stairs to find your view is blocked by the back of a large theatrical prop representing a classical Chinese landscape; you see its two-by-four frame and the rough edges of its papier-mâché covering. This strange backstage sight highlights the artificiality and theatricality of the dramatic installation just beyond it. Nine realistic tigers, made of fiberglass and covered with meticulously painted hide, are pierced by hundreds of arrows and hang from the ceiling in various dynamic poses. In fear, surprise, pain, or belligerence, they crouch, leap, and writhe. They move in the opposite direction of the cars, which are in the gallery parallel to this one.

Cai has said his thinking about the work was shaped by the story of *Wu Song the Tiger Slayer*, taken from a Chinese literary classic, *Outlaws of the Marsh*, also variously known as Tales of the Water Margin and All Men are Brothers. Set in the final years of the Song Dynasty (1101-1125), it tells the tales of virtuous men and women who were forced to become "bandits" chiefly due to an oppressive and corrupt society. Its themes of heroism, fraternity, honor, justice, and courage are well known to Chinese schoolchildren. Wu Song was a bandit who passed through a village that was terrorized by a man-eating tiger. In a moment of sudden courage, he decided to hunt down the marauding tiger: fortifying himself with spirits, Wu Song ventured into the mountain. To his great surprise, he was able to kill the tiger and thus save the village. From this inopportune encounter, the character has become the paragon of heroism in China. Of course, the Chinese are not the only people who once equated killing tigers, lions, and certain other wild animals with courage and strength. Cai was greatly affected by an ancient Egyptian image of the pharaohs hunting lions. But during Cai's lifetime, the way society regards the killing of tigers has completely changed. Killing a tiger today is criminal, wasteful, and cruel. Who has attacked these tigers – a hero or a villain? And what have the tigers done – if anything – to bring about such a fierce attack?

Cai used arrows like those that pierce the nine tigers in several earlier works, including one from 1998 called *Borrowing Your Enemy's Arrows*. For that work, a wooden boat struck with 3,000 arrows is suspended in mid-air, like the tigers at MASS MoCA. In a 2002 interview with Octavio Zaya, Cai had this to say about the arrows:

> Even though you feel that the arrows symbolize wounding and pain, at the same time the boat is uplifted; the feathers of the arrows enable it, as it were, to take flight. So there's a beautiful contradiction which resembles elements in Chinese martial arts. To describe it in basic terms, in Western boxing if the opponent is hit in the face hard enough he falls, so it's easy to decide who's won. In Chinese martial arts it's much more complex, more internal. The exchanges are more subtle, often using the opponent's own force to defeat him. [1]

Several key formal devices appear repeatedly in *Inopportune's* four linked works. The first is circularity: the fact that the first and last cars are identical implies that the explosion is a closed circuit traversed continually; the repeating loop of the video has the same implication; the ellipse in the drawing is common symbol for continuity; and the parallel placement of the tigers and cars also suggests it. These cycles point to eternal and universal questions rather than momentary and local ones.

Like circularity and repetition, explosions are central to three of the works, and though the tigers do not explode, the arrows that pierce them mirror the light rods that jut out of the hanging cars. One receives and the other discharges a force. Explosions have been a central part of Cai's creative practice since the mid-1980s, when he left China for Japan, where he lived from 1986 - 1995. Although some critics have explained Cai's experiments with gunpowder and other explosives from a biographical point of view (there is an important Chinese army base positioned across the strait from Taiwan, and Cai saw many fighter planes and frequently heard cannon shots while he lived there [2]), the use of fireworks and other explosives derives not only from his hometown but from China as a whole.

In my hometown every significant social occasion of any kind, good or bed – weddings, funerals, the birth of a baby, a new home – is marked by the explosion of firecrackers … Firecrackers are like the town crier, announcing whatever's going on in the town… I saw gunpowder used in both good ways and bad, in destruction and reconstruction. Gunpowder was invented in China as a by-product of alchemy. It is still called "fire medicine" because it was accidentally created during an attempt to produce a medicine. [3]

For Cai, explosions – whether from gun powder, fireworks, or even the atomic bomb – go beyond any national context. Their origins in alchemy invoke curative, transformative power and cosmic questions. Even a small firecracker for Cai is connected to much larger releases of energy, even to the Big Bang.

When I came to Japan my encounters with the theories of twentieth-century astrophysics were very significant to me. The concepts of the Big Bang, black holes, the birth of stars, what is beyond the universe, time tunnels, how to leap over great distances of time and space and dialogue with something infinitely far away – these ideas were still not commonly in circulation in China at the time. They were an eye-opener for me. At the same time, many of these ideas have similarities with traditional Chinese views, with which I was familiar, of metaphysics and the universe. [4]

In fact, most of Cai's aesthetic choices are rooted in venerable and robust Chinese artistic traditions. His recurrent use of the number nine (cars and tigers) as well as the long, horizontal format in the installations and the video can be found in the ancient art of Chinese scroll painting. (His father is a classically trained artist whose *100* Tigers scroll will hang in Cai's exhibition.) Paradigmatic of this tradition is a 13th century scroll in the collection of the Museum of Fine Arts, Boston. Chen Rong's *Nine Dragons* is the oldest and finest such scroll extant and points to a practice that pre- and postdates it by nearly a thousand years. [5] Chen's *Nine Dragons* was inspired by a 10th century scroll called *Nine Deer*, which was in turn inspired by an 8th century example *Nine Horses*, and so on. [6] Cai's work rest on a foundation of tens

Cai Guo-Qiang, *Borrowing Your Enemy's Arrows*, 1998
P.S. 1 Contemporary Art Center, New York.
Wooden boat, straw, bamboo, arrows, flags, fan
ca. 33 ft. long
Collection of Museum of Modern Art

of thousands of nine animal scrolls made throughout the centuries. Wu Tung's interpretation of this scroll in his 1997 exhibition catalogue *Tales from the Land of Dragons* could easily be applied to the nine cars in *Inopportune*. He writes: "The varied expressions of the dragons, their movements and interplay with different elements in nature . . . are manifestations of the *Dao*. (The contrasts in the work) accord with the fundamental Daoist concept of life as the interaction of two forces: *yin* (the negative, receptive, or feminine principle) and *yang* (the positive, creative, or masculine principle)." [7]

To Western eyes, the use of nine cars to represent nine *moments* in a single unfolding event seems to draw on the work of pioneering photographer Eadweard Muybridge (1880 - 1904). Muybridge fa–mously invented stop-action photography as a way of settling the question of whether all four of a galloping horse's hooves left the ground simultaneously. (They do.) But Wu reveals a far older Chinese source. "The nine dragons in the scroll," he notes, "may also be interpreted as one entity experiencing

nine transformations in shape, emotion, age, and wisdom." [9] Commentary on this scroll as early as the 14th century offers this interpretation, as well as the belief that the number nine represents the positive, creative, masculine element of *yang*.

In describing his work in general, Cai has said that "Art can transcend time and space, and achieve something that science cannot. The job of the artist is to create such time/space tunnels." [9] Crucial to the creation of a "time/space tunnel" such as we see in *Inopportune* is the sense of being in a dreamscape that, though tethered to reality, has gone outside of it. Like the number nine, the long scroll format, and the fireworks, the evocation of a dream state is part of an ancient tradition. For example, the Boston dragon scroll has incredibly rare colophon added by the artist in which he recounts that he was able to paint the dragons while he was in an intoxicated state of mind. "The creative process recorded in both text and image reflects certain mind-altering experiences and insights long associated with Daoist transcendental practices." [10] Even Wu Song the Tiger

Slayer's drunkenness during his encounter with the man-eating tiger should be seen in this light, not as folly or bad luck, but as an altered, otherworldly consciousness. It is into this state of consciousness that *Inopportune* invites us.

Although these works derive in part from long-lived Eastern traditions, they also reverberate with Western ones. After all, *Inopportune* was made in the West, for a Western audience, by an artist active in the Western art world for over a decade. A salient feature of Cai's installation for a Western viewer is his use of spectacular light and color. Pulsing lights transform the hanging cars in dramatic, even sublime fashion. The same is true for the glorious, baroque, enveloping use of colored light in the video *Illusion*. Where else in art do these dazzling, spectacular lights appear? Where has this kind of beauty been married with feelings of terror as it is here?

One clue to answering this question can be found in the only poster on Cai's studio wall: a painting by El Greco from his 2003 retrospective at the Metropolitan Museum of Art. [11]

El Greco's paintings are paradigmatic of the way Western artists have used glorious lights and colors, and *The Adoration of the Name of Jesus* (c.1578), which was included in the Metropolitan exhibition, is paradigmatic of El Greco's painting. The painting shows the heavens opening in an astonishing burst of light to reveal the Greek name of Jesus (IHS) shimmering like the sun. Piebald angels wheel in the sky, which reverberates with color. In the foreground, the Pope, the Doge of Venice, and King Phillip II of Spain are shown kneeling in adoration of the name of Jesus, which was believed to have power over infidels. On the right, heretics are swallowed by a dark monstrous beast, swimming in a sea of smoke. The symbolism of the marvelous light could not be clearer: it is the light of heaven, of Jesus, salvation for the good and just.

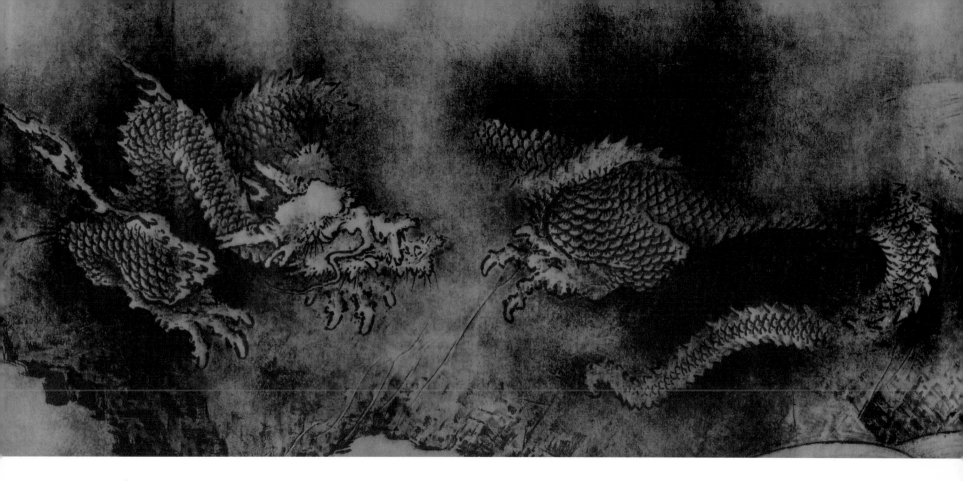

Chen Rong, Chinese, first half of the 13th century, *Nine Dragons* (Detail), 1244
Chinese, Southern Song dynasty
Ink and touches of red on paper
Photo: Museum of Fine Arts, Boston. Francis Gardner Curtis Fund. Photograph © Museum of Fine Arts, Boston

Similar use of light can be found in sculptural works; Gianlorenzo Bernini's *Ecstasy of Saint Teresa* (1647-1652) is the most obvious example. Installed in the Cornaro Chapel in the transept of Santa Maria della Vittoria, in Rome, the famous life-sized sculpture captures the saint's vision of an angel, "his face so aflame that he appeared to be one of the highest ranks of angels, who seem to be all on fire," who plunged an arrow into her heart. The pain she suffered was made bearable only by the mystic ecstasy she experienced, represented by a giant starburst made of golden rods lit by a hidden window above her, which strongly resembles the tubes of light emanating from the cars in *Inopportune*.

The symbolism of the glorious light of heaven is ubiquitous in the West. Nearly very museum, every cathedral, every church displays paintings, sculptures, and stained glass with this as a central motif. The connection of the glory of God, and in particular of righteousness, with spectacular light and of evil with darkness is ingrained in Western viewers. (Even in contemporary popular culture this is the case. Countless movies use a car chase followed by a giant explosion as a way to restore order to an unbalanced world. The villains die, the heroes are saved.) The inclination to understand this particular form of intense colored light as symbolic of righteousness deeply complicates Cai's installation and video. To whom does this righteousness belong? The installation is disturbingly mute on the subject, forcing us, the viewers, to struggle with the question alone.

Inopportune poses questions whose scope is eternal rather than immediate, universal rather than local, and metaphysical rather than mundane. But those questions unequivocally take the form of a car bomb. As this essay is being written in the winter of 2004, car bombs are immediate, local, daily concerns, addressed in every news cycle. And although Cai, like many successful artists, is a citizen of the world, his family was at home in lower Manhattan on September 11, 2001. Terrorism is not only abstract and metaphysical for him, it is also personal.

We live in complicated times. Over the last several years, religious and cultural strife has penetrated the consciousness of Americans in a new way. Since the

Chen Rong, Chinese, first half of the 13th century, *Nine Dragons,* 1244
Chinese, Southern Song dynasty
Ink and touches of red on paper, 46.3 x 1069.4 cm (18 1/4 x 431 5/8 in.)
Photo: Museum of Fine Arts, Boston. Francis Gardner Curtis Fund. Photograph © Museum of Fine Arts, Boston

Muybridge, Eadweard (1830-1904)
Transverse-Gallop, photograph, 1887. From *Animals in Motion.*
Photo credit : Image Select / Art Resource, NY

Cai Guo-Qiang, *Inopportune Stage Two, 2004:* Nine
cars and sequenced multi-channel tube lights
MASS MoCA Commission

terrorist attacks of September 2001, every car bomb in a faraway place seems a little nearer, instilling in us the idea that it could happen here. It is a difficult, but important, time to make art. Art in general, and Cai Guo-Qiang's *Inopportune* in particular, creates a space, a time, and imagery in and around which to gather our thoughts, without prescribing what those thoughts should be. This is a difficult concept to grapple with, almost as difficult as the idea that an explosion can be beautiful. In the U.S. today, these ideas feel untimely, inappropriate, unsettling – even inopportune – which, for Cai, makes them urgently in need of contemplation and perfectly suited to his art.

Endnotes

1. Octavio Zaya et al, Cai Guo-Qiang (New York: Phadion, 2002) p.28

2. Zaya, p.14

3. Ibid

4. Zaya, p.16

5. Wu Tung, Tales from the Land of Dragons: 1,000 Years of Chinese Painting (Boston: Museum of Fine Arts, 1997) p.197

6. Ibid

7. Wu, p.199

8. Ibid

9. Zaya, p.17

10. Wu, p.198

11. Conversation with Jennifer Ma, September 2004.

Bernini, Gian Lorenzo (1598-1680)
Ecstasy of St. Theresa
Location : Cornaro Chapel, S. Maria della
Vittoria, Rome, Italy
Photo credit : Scala / Art Resource, NY

Greco, El (1541-1614)
The Dream of Phillip II
Location : El Escorial, Spain
Photo credit : Scala / Art Resource, NY

Cai Guo-Qiang, *Study for Inopportune: Stage One,* 2004
Fluorescent highlighter and ink on paper

Of Terror and Tigers:
Reflections on Cai Guo-Qiang's *Inopportune*

ROBERT POGUE HARRISON

Stanford University

Inopportune is an artwork that erupts from out of the core of our bewildered age. Or maybe one should say: it reveals the explosive core of the age from which it erupts – an age in which we carry on our lives as if the framework supporting them were not under a constant threat of fulmination. The nature of this threat is obscure, like the artwork that confronts us here with its luminous enigma. *Inopportune* leaves one perplexed, uneasy, and in a state of wonder. One does not know what to make of it, or how to translate its impact into words or ideas. Indeed, impact is everything here. And yet we look again and see that beneath the deliberate aggression in the narrative of these objects, the work as a whole, in its four-part installation, achieves an aesthetic resolution that opens up a space of reflective calm at the heart of its upheavals. It is as if the artist enlisted the tactics of shock and awe in order to call on us to think. If we choose to respond to that call emanating from the fireworks, we find ourselves thinking not only about *Inopportune* – its complex articulation, its logic, its meaning – but also about the terrorized and terrorizing era to which we, along with the artwork, belong. For this is a work that, by calling on us to think, places us squarely at the center of the times – or at the center, as it were, of Times Square.

These cars, for example. Or rather, *this* car. For surely it is the same car in an odyssey of successive frozen frames that is on display here. Nonetheless, there are nine real cars in the room, each identical to the others. What kind of *e pluribus unum* is this? The least we can say about a car bomb is that it shatters the principle of identity by annihilating the vehicle of its delivery. Here the car preserves its integrity through the process of igniting. So this is not really an explosion after all. As the artist himself has declared, it is more like a dream image than a representation. But what does it mean to dream a car bomb? Dreams are for the most part harmless, while a car bomb is anything but harmless for those who find themselves in the vicinity of its detonation. In *Inopportune: Stage One*, the catastrophe is at once silent, beautiful and innocuous, for the self-same car remains in tact after its tumultuous ride through the air. This is disturbing. It unsettles. We know that the explosion took place – that it is taking place – yet its effects, cancelled out at the end of the trajectory, are consigned to the oblivion of dreams or the order of illusion.

Illusion? The second installation of *Inopportune* features a 90-second video entitled exactly that: *Illusion*. A car superimposed on the scene enters Times Square from the left side of the screen, explodes in the middle of the square, and then returns again, repeating its action in a continuous loop. Here too the explosion is clearly harmless, for it has no effect on the bustle and rush of traffic in the square. It would seem, then, that the car bomb goes off somewhere in the phantasmagoria of the viewer's mind, that it is precisely as the title says: an illusion. But what do car bombs, and the terrorism with which they are associated, have to do with illusion? There is nothing illusory about terrorist acts, to be sure, yet the terror they unleash after their impact feeds off the natural extravagance of the human imagination, which exceeds reality on all sides. A single act of terrorism can turn all places, all beings, all people, into potential targets, thanks to what Jean Baudrillard calls the "spirit of terrorism," with its vast imaginary and symbolic reach.[1] Andrew Mitchell puts it well when he writes: "Terror brings about an alteration in the very mode of being of reality; the real is now the terrorized. The change has already taken place, and this regardless of whether an attack comes or not…. The effectiveness of terror lies in the threat, not the attack." One could say that *Illusion* puts in motion a visual allegory of the imaginary threat that hangs over reality. What we see in the video is *not* the imaginary destruction of Times Square but the square as transformed into the site of a potential holocaust. The car that enters the scene and explodes is the visible correlate of the invisible threat in and through which terrorism alters reality even as it leaves it intact. In this respect, the illusion in question is not that a car bomb has exploded in the square, it is that nothing has really taken place after all. *Illusion* reveals that Times Square in a post-September 11 era is no longer the Times Square of old. Its identity, or self-sameness in time, has been exploded – not by a car bomb as such, but by its specter.

The specter of terrorism has a way of moving through closed doors, insinuating itself into our secret fears, our vulnerabilities, our unavowed guilt, our existential dread. The statistical risks of becoming a casualty of a terrorist attack on American soil are on the whole extremely minimal, if not infinitesimal, yet look at how we quake with anxiety! Listen to our cries for more security measures, for more "homeland security"! How ready we are to trade in our cherished liberties for the sake – or for the illusion – of safety. This is far from harmless. The question that we must ask, that we are called on by *Inopportune* to ask, is one that puts us at a certain risk. What is it about the times that renders us so easily terrified? What is the deeper source of our perturbation, figured here in dream-like images?

It is the age itself that terrifies us. It is not because there are terrorists that we live in a terrifying age. It is because we live in a terrifying age that terrorism can wreck havoc with our insecurities. If Times Square seems like the ideal target of a terrorist attack, it is because it is charged with a heavy symbolic load of the global network that has transformed, that is to say devastated, our relation to beings and to the earth to which we once belonged. It is the monstrous complexity, relentless expansion and sinister death-drive of that planetary network that fill us with dread.

The spectacle of "what man has made of man," to borrow a phrase from Wordsworth, is altogether awesome. That we are still able to experience a tremor of terror in the face of the technological forces that have put the earth and the totality of its resources on standing-reserve for human ordering and exploitation is an indication that the human in us has not been entirely extinguished, that we have not yet been fully transhumanized, or at least that our memory of being human has not been completely abolished. Soon we will no longer be able to feel even such a tremor, and that is what is most dreadful of all.

The age of terror is the age of "technicity," a word that the German philosopher Martin Heidegger coined to name the "essence of technology," which in itself is nothing technological. While we presume to author, direct and regulate our technologies, human beings do not control the inner will that drives us to amass more and more technical capability and to "enframe" all beings in an ever-expanding order of distribution and consumption. "Technicity in its essence is something that man does not master

by his own power." [3] Heidegger adds that its will to unconditional domination operates not only beyond the control of man, but, as it unearths the earth, wrests nature's secrets from their concealment, and devastates whatever lies in its way, it operates for the most part against us – against what is human in us. The terror is that we are its agents, that we are the agents of its dehumanization. As it strives to abolish all distance and singularity across the planet and to render all things available and disposable, technicity turns human beings into resources along with everything else it places on standing-reserve for future utilization. ""Man is the 'most important raw material'," writes Heidegger, "because he remains the subject of all consumption. He does this in such a way that he lets his will be unconditionally equated with this process, and thus at the same time become the 'object' of the abandonment of Being." [4] In their abandonment by Being, beings remain denatured, groundless, in a word terrorized. A world from which Being has taken flight is no longer a world in any human sense. Indeed, "the 'world' has become an unworld as a consequence of the abandonment of beings by the truth of Being" (ibid). What does *Inopportune* have to do with this unworld, or with the planetary movement that, independently of human governance, is bringing about an absolutely technical state – and soon, an absolutely bio-technical state – on the earth?

The least we can say is that the work arises as a response to it. In his interview in 1969 with the German magazine *Der Spiegel*, Heidegger was asked: "What must be mastered in this case? Everything is functioning. More and more electric power companies are being built. Production is up. In highly technologized parts of the earth, people are well cared for. We are living in a state of prosperity. What really is lacking to us?" To which Heidegger answered: "Everything is functioning. That is precisely what is awesome [or terror-inducing], that everything functions, that the functioning propels everything more and more toward further functioning, and that technicity increasingly dislodges man and uproots him from the earth" [5]. *Illusion* offers a flash of insight into the awesome nature of "everything functioning." What is eerie about Times Square in the video is not so much the spectral car whose explosion is superimposed on the scene. It's that the explosion is feckless, that business goes on as usual, that the cars and people continue to circulate, in short, that seemingly nothing can resist or obstruct the implacable functioning of the global network, of which Times Square is here a symbolic node.

The paradox of the age is that the ordering and enframing drive of planetary technicity in fact violently disrupts and disworlds the world. The times to which we belong are in that sense radically combustible, and Cai Guo-Qiang has understood this as radically as any contemporary artist. The effects of this combustion upon our lived worlds, and upon the earth as a whole, are evoked in the third part of the installation, *Nine Cars Drawing*, with its image of an ellipse made by exploding gunpowder on the paper's surface. In its form, this ellipse is essentially cosmic, recalling among other things the earth's orbit around the sun. Yet the title links it to the exploding car of *Inopportune:*

Stage One, as if to suggest that what takes place in *Inopportune: Stage One* has planetary repercussions, that the impact of the car's detonation in "Stage One" goes well beyond the single event under depiction (hence the "stage one" appellation).

If nothing else, *Inopportune* forces us to reflect on the nature of combustion, its effects on both the human and natural world. From a strictly theoretical point of view, one could say that "Stage One" does not depict a car bomb, but merely offers a fantastical image of the internal combustion that allows cars to function at all. In other words, it is the car in its everyday functioning that is the bomb. And who, looking at things dispassionately, not to say ecologically, could in good conscience deny this? For a century and more we in the west have wedded ourselves to the automobile, have transformed the very fabric of our habitats to meet the demands of the automobile, have dug deep into the earth and seas in order to extract the liquefied fossils that fuel the automobile, have enthralled the rest of the world to the automobile. The car has on the whole terrorized the earth, and

its work is far from done. One day – if human history has such a future – we will look back to the era of the automobile as something quite insane, something fundamentally inexplicable. Meanwhile we fight to the death to defend our right to remain enslaved to its demands.

Works of art have the power to reveal the being of things in singular ways. *Inopportune* reveals that internal combustion involves an external combustion that impacts outward, into the world. The most intriguing part of the installation is *Inopportune: Stage Two*, with its nine arrow-riddled tigers in various positions of tension and stress. What are we to make of this work, especially in relation to the other parts of the installation? In her companion piece in this volume, Laura Heon discusses in eloquent fashion the traditional Chinese subtexts in Cai's use of the tiger and arrow motifs, pointing out the parallel placement of the tigers and cars. About the tigers she writes: "The arrows that pierce them mirror the light rods that jut out of the hanging cars. One receives and the other discharges a force." If one considers the 14th century

Chinese literary work, *Outlaws of the Marsh*, to which these tigers apparently allude – a work in which the bandit hero Wu Song slays a man-eating tiger that had been terrorizing a village – then one is tempted to see in *Inopportune's* final image the slaying and defeat of the terrorist forces evoked in the preceding parts. Hence the installation would conclude on an uplifting note, to the effect that we (whoever "we" may be) will triumph in some heroic manner over the terror that explodes our cars and disrupts our world. However, in the line of reasoning that I have been pursuing here – call it a free engagement with the work at the level of speculative reflection – the arrows figure as the outward impact of the cars' light rods on the tigers themselves. If the tiger in *Outlaws of the Marsh* was a force of terror, here the tigers are creatures of pure passion, victims of the violent external combustion of the internal combustion engine. Whatever they may otherwise symbolize, these tigers are embodiments of animal life, and in that respect they appear here as figures for the natural world, which the planetary unleashing of human power terrorizes. In their passion we see a figure for the suffering of the animal kingdom as a whole in the age of technicity.

Such a hypothesis holds little comfort, to be sure, yet the purpose of art is not to console but to rouse us from the half-slumber in which we get on with our everyday, practical lives. In some cases this means arousing in us a sense of terror and pity. *Inopportune* does precisely that. In "Stage One," the terror; in "Stage Two," the pity. Art's vocation has been linked to terror and pity ever since Aristotle defined the art of tragedy as the "catharis" or release of these emotions. Art does not domesticate terror in pity; rather, it transfigures terror in the beautiful. Such transfiguration, which preserves the power of what it appropriates, is clearly at work here. *Inopportune* reminds us of the terror of beauty; and in so doing creates the possibility of a pity without condescension, a pity fraught with genuine, self-referential dread. In the first of his *Duino Elegies* Rilke declares: "Beauty is nothing / but the beginning of terror we can just barely endure, / and we admire it so is because it calmly disdains / to destroy us." [6] *Inopportune* calls for this sort of strange admiration. It is explosive and violent, like the age from whose core it erupts, yet it is also pervaded by an underlying, disdainful calm. This is the kind of beautiful calm that only art knows how to secure amid great commotion. In precisely such a calm, which calls thinking forth into the presence of terror, lies the work's challenge to the convulsive and disfiguring forces of the age – forces that, when left to themselves, put all thoughtfulness to flight, leaving us stunned and bewildered. It takes an art at least as powerful as the forces of the age itself to open a space of thoughtfulness in their midst, for it is only from out of the terror that the powers of rescue can arise.

Endnotes

1   See Jean Baudrillard's *The Spirit of Terrorism*, trans. Chris Turner (London & New York: Verso, 2002). All four essays in this excellent collection are pertinent to the theme of my meditation, but see especially "Hypothesis on Terrorism" (pp. 49-84).

2   The quote comes from Andrew Mitchell's superb essay, "Heidegger and Terrorism," forthcoming in the *Research in Phenomenology*, vol. 35 (Fall, 2005).

3   Martin Heidegger, interview with *Der Spiegel*, "'Only a God Can Save Us': The *Spiegel* interview (1966)," trans. William J. Richardson, in *Heidegger: The Man and the Thinker*, ed. Thomas Sheehan (Chicago: Precedent Publishing, Inc., 1981), p. 56.

4   Martin Heidegger, interview with *Der Spiegel*.

5   Martin Heidegger, *The End of Philosophy*, ed. and trans. Joan Stambaugh (New York: Harper & Row, Publishers, 1973) p. 104.

6   Rainer Maria Rilke, *Duino Elegies*, trans. C. F. MacIntyre (Berkeley, Los Angeles, London: University of California Press, 1961), p. 3.

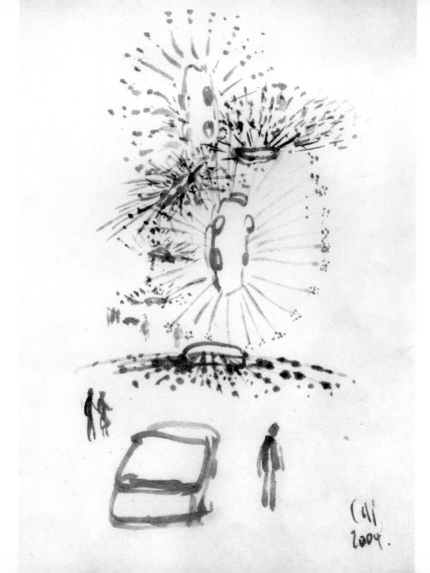

Cai Guo-Qiang, *Study for Inopportune: Stage One,* 2004
Pen and ink on paper

Cai Guo-Qiang
Inopportune

Cai Guo-Qiang, *Study for Inopportune: Stage Two,* 2004
Collage of photographs and ink on paper

Planning the installation of Inopportune at MASS MoCA, Summer 2004

Installing *Inopportune* at MASS MoCA, December 2004

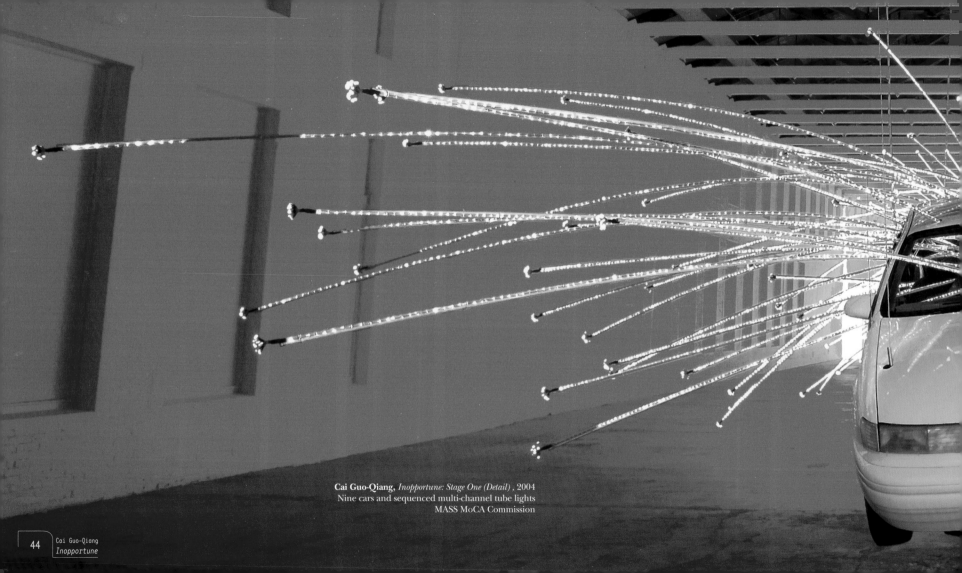

Cai Guo-Qiang, *Inopportune: Stage One (Detail)* , 2004
Nine cars and sequenced multi-channel tube lights
MASS MoCA Commission

Cai Guo-Qiang
Inopportune

Cai Guo-Qiang, *Illusion,* 2004
Three-channel DVD projection (97 seconds, looped); car and spent fireworks
Videography by John Borst
Edited by Lauren Petty
MASS MoCA Commission

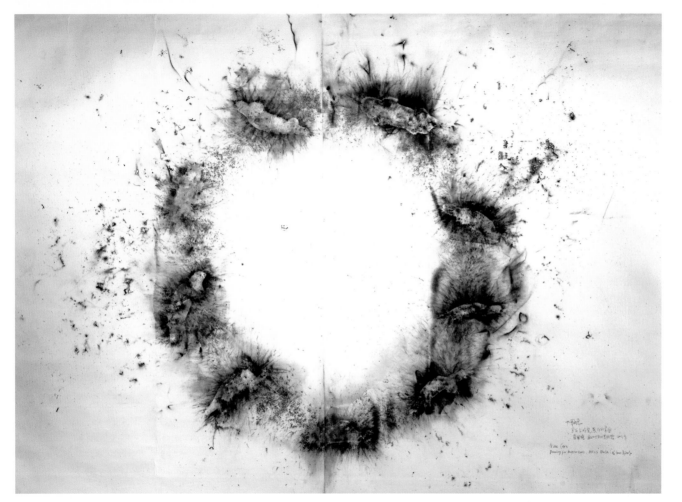

Cai Guo-Qiang, *Nine Cars,* 2004
Exploded gunpowder on paper
MASS MoCA Commission

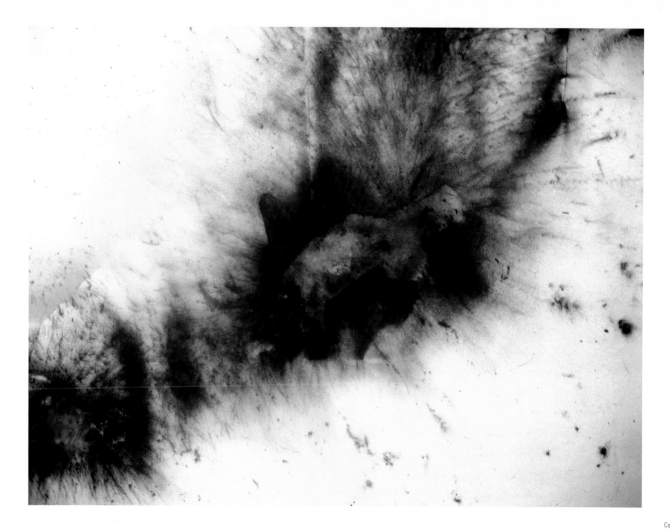

Cai Guo-Qiang, *Nine Cars (Detail),* 2004
Exploded gunpowder on paper
MASS MoCA Commission

Cai Guo-Qiang
Inopportune

I wish it never happened

Cai Guo-Qiang interviewed
by Jennifer Ma, director
of Cai Studio

December 2004

Ma: Let's start by talking about your exhibition at MASS MoCA. This installation feels different from your works of the last five years, which are subversive, but amusing. This one is inappropriate and anti-mainstream. Your manner is sober.

Cai: As a whole, an audience looking at these works may feel a little uncomfortable, but there are still ingredients of humor, such as a car flipping over in mid-air, a tiger pierced with arrows, a stage prop mountain. It's still delightful.

There are two inopportune or, as you say, "inappropriate" elements; one concerns 9/11 and the Iraq war – in particular the one-sided landslide of condemnation of terrorism. The other element is that, since the '90s, artistic circles have been less concerned with sociopolitical issues. Against the backdrop of the condemnation of terrorism and my own tendency toward lighthearted art, my car bombs are politically incorrect and can be said to be "inopportune." This includes killing tigers. In the past when man was weak, it was heroic; but now man, with his flood of weapons,

Cai Guo-Qiang, *Study for Inopportune: Stage Two*, 2004
Pen and ink on paper

is like a torrential flood, and the number of animals has decreased. From the perspective of environmental protection, killing tigers is abusive and inopportune. The work will trigger other concerns, and the viewers' disquiet concerning violence will interrupt the beauty and elegance of the work.

Ma: Before your video of a car bomb in Times Square, *Illusion*, was installed, it generated some debate at MASS MoCA. Some people wondered if the work would appear to exploit traumatic events.

Cai: I thought about this before it happened, that some people would be unhappy. I already knew that the work would cause an emotional reaction. However, the museum staff may have exaggerated the directness of my work. My starting point was not 9/11 itself, but the unidirectionality of culture and thought following that event. Before 9/11, the attitude toward other religions – and especially the issue of how developed Western countries look upon Islamic society – was more nuanced and open to debate. After 9/11, people no longer discussed these issues,

but instead demonstrated a near universal revulsion toward the display of endless suicide bombings by Arabic youth. Art cannot directly change society, but it can give people a new perspective for contemplation. Consequently, these works collectively cause people emotional and intellectual discomfort.

Ma: Do you consider it your role to counter the American audience's singular point of view with aesthetics?

Cai: Generally speaking, most art is not politically correct; otherwise it would simply be propaganda. Art stands more in a blurred and troubled region. Yet, it often induces people to observe the two sides of a situation, and causes people discomfort, which elicits further reflection.

Ma: The car piece exists in a very long space. It takes the form of Chinese scroll painting. You also show your father's scroll paintings, which invite a spatial reading.

Cai: The space in the museum is 18 x 100 meters (55 x 275'). It resembles a highway and suits the car explosion project. The tiger work developed along side it. These two works unfurl like scrolls. In contrast to looking at a Western painting, the method used to read a scroll also includes the extension of time revealed section by section as the scroll unfurls. It can show the change of seasons or passage through a landscape. Scroll paintings and folding screens are similar, mobile, especially because the size can be changed according to the space. The composition of an oil painting is integral and cannot do this. A scroll painting can always be displayed a section at a time; each section is integral in itself. When the space is large, a folding screen can be outstretched; when it is small, it can be folded up. Ancient Chinese painters were fastidious about the relationship between space and people, and as the viewer moves about the work, about the difference in feeling and experience that is brought on. A long folding screen cannot be taken in in one glance; if you walk in one direction, you see a spring breeze over the southern bank of an emerald river; walk the other direction and waves ripple on the surface of a pond as if the wind has carried them with it, as if the wind is walking over the small bridge over the pool. There is a sense of process occurring in time; it needs the process to be read. "Readable" is a description that suits Chinese art. In ancient times it was not called "looking at a painting;" it was called "reading a painting." This is a very contemporary idea. Long scroll paintings are even more so meant to be "read." The right hand rolls, the left hand unrolls, several meters of reading pass as if traveling ten thousand miles of road: this is painting in time.

My installations have consistently pursued a temporal fluidity, in contrast to the stylistic freedom I allow myself. However, my works in essence contain these characteristics: a participatory nature and a flow of time. They need process to be read and understood.

Ma: *Inopportune: Stage One*, in particular, requires viewers to walk through and look for themselves.

Cai: Spectators enter into a disorderly pile of objects: an explosion of lights, the cars piled up together, a

Cai Ruiqing (Cai Guo-Qiang's father)
Painting of One Hundred Tigers, 1993
Ink on paper mounted on silk
Courtesy of the artist

Cai Guo-Qiang, *Transient Rainbow*, 2002
New York, USA
Commissioned by Museum of Modern Art

Cai Guo-Qiang,
Light Cycle: Explosion Project
for Central Park, 2004. New York, USA
Commissioned by Creative Time

Cai Guo-Qiang, *An Arbitrary History: River,* 2001
Musee d'Art Contemporain de Lyon, Lyon, France, 2001
Collection of the Artist

profusion of colors. When reading the work, the first car appears to be driving normally; the second car lifts off the ground with a bang. I understand explosions. At the beginning the light is white, a pure intense color; the force of impact causes the car to float; then the air combusts; it turns red, the temperature appears to rise (in fact, it falls); the car ascends and tumbles in mid-air; a profusion of color emerges and turns into a fiery display of pyrotechnics; afterwards it turns pink like a dream. As it descends to the ground, its plumage is spread out like a bird, and it is blue. The entire process must be read by the audience walking along its side. The cars are like freeze frames at points in time; nine cars make the story of one car. The body walking by is like a roll of film turning, allowing one to see the movement of the installation.

Ma: *Inopportune: Stage One* and *Illusion* feel similar in their proliferation of disorderly color. The former is very physical, the cars are real. Although the explosions are made from light tubes, they are still substantial. The video is clearly artificial, but the audience has a stronger reaction to it. Why?

Cai: Times Square in New York has an intense materiality and a feeling of danger that cuts through the flesh. The people in the video, surrounded by a debauchery of color, are oblivious to the car bomb happening right in front of them. The car repeatedly exploding is like a phantom. The video was deliberately shot from eye level; it is as if we are seeing a never-ending cycle of car bombs passing through time and space in Times Square. It is a kind of hallucination – an "illusion," as the title says. *Illusion* and *Inopportune* have different visual impacts, shapes, colors, lights, rhythms, and speeds. But I can't say which work deserves deeper discussion.

Ma: The visceral power of photography and video is well recognized. Everybody knows that this media can be as artificial and subjective as painting, but we still comprehend photography and video as if they were real.

Cai: In the past, we understood war through text rather than video. We had to imagine the city being destroyed, bodies spread over the ground, and we were terrified of war. In 1991, we saw the Gulf War for ourselves on television, and it reassured us to think we had a real conception of what war was like. But, in fact, this is even more dangerous than before, since what we see now has been processed and selected. We may know the status of English and American deaths, but the loss of thousands or hundreds of thousands of Iraqi lives cannot be read through the camera lens. The place we see on TV has sunlight; people can be seen walking on the road. The audience believes they have experienced and understood for themselves what is actually happening there – that video tells the truth. This is very dangerous.

Ma: Are you altering reality in your work? Because an explosion has not occurred in Times Square.

Cai: The danger lies in the fact that it seems to have, and seems not to have, happened.

Ma: Are you talking about the government's manipulation of media, or your artistic strategy?

Cai: After an event occurs, we often think, "I wish it never happened." The work is called *Illusion*, and our illusions stem from our age. The video is more direct than the car installation or the tigers, more connected to the current situation. This trend is reflected in some of my other works. For the Sao Paolo biennial, for example, 10,000 objects collected at security checks were stuck into an airplane: knives, nail-clippers, scissors, and forks. These objects do not come from enemies but from us. Everybody has weapons, everybody is the enemy. In a war it is difficult to distinguish the enemy from oneself; it is confused. Terrorists appear and disappear mysteriously like ghosts, which places the right and wrong of a situation in wider and subtler relationships. Consequently, art has also changed.

Ma: The simplicity of terrorists' means – like box cutters – relates to your work. For example, the video is simple and crude, made with three rented camera lenses and a simple rig that clamped the cameras in place. It was recorded in one night. A truck towed the car filled with kids' fireworks. It may be called low-tech.

Cai Guo-Qiang, *Bon Voyage: 10,000 Collectables from the Airport,* 2004
Sao Paulo Biennial, Brazil
Collection of the Artist

Cai: The terrorists used knives, in a simple and primitive method, but they went through a lot of training and preparation, like learning civil aviation law. Many artists are like this. My work looks reckless, but in fact it is somewhat contrary to that. Some people are good at doing complex things simply; some people are good at presenting simple things using complex, highly technical, detailed, and precise forms. My works are generally simple and easy, easy to participate in. This is related to my background; I grew up in a small city, you could say as an Asian peasant. My values, sense of dimension, degree of material treatment, sense of weight and temperature, are all intimately connected to my background.

You are right that I often use simple technology and crude materials. The light tubes are from the streets, the old cars were painted white; for the tigers, grass bales were covered with papier-mâché and the fur was glued on.

The Times Square video used a very simple editing and shooting method. I wanted to see if I could do something new with this widely used form of video. I knew it wouldn't be easy, because I don't really know how to work with it. I was just giving it a try. Although it communicated the sociopolitical issues I wanted to express, I didn't find anything especially significant in terms of means. I was just feeling my way around. I'm actually not too fond of video, since I don't like relying on machinery to indirectly convey what I wish to. I prefer direct objects. But I felt that this project should use this format; and since I don't really understand video, I didn't play with technique, just took the simplest approach. museum often provide these things. They are like a climate. You've spent time tilling and fertilizing the soil, sowing and weeding for a long time, but you must wait for the right season. Different museums provide different climates.

Ma: You often discuss methodology, in particular your use of Chinese traditions like Chinese medicine and feng-shui. In this case, I feel that you are responding to the methodologies of terrorism.

Cai: My work begins with things I observe and am interested in; this, then, gradually becomes the desire to produce a work. For example, I make explosions, so I pay attention to explosions. I can imagine the methods used and mental state of the suicide bombers. In a crowd, the police make them raise their hands. As soon as their fingers separate, the positive or negative electrodes connect, detonation, a simple action. Before igniting an artwork, I am sometimes nervous, yet terrorists face death unflinchingly. Along with the sympathy we hold for the victims, I also have compassion for the young men and women who commit the act. Artists can sympathize with the other possibility, present issues from someone else's point of view. The work of art comes into being because our society has this predicament. Artists do not pronounce it good or bad.

But, having said that, the answer to your question is no, I have not intentionally researched the methodology of terrorism for my work. Terrorists make noise in the East, but attack in the West. They switched from assassination of presidents to striking the most symbolic of objects like the Twin Towers, to attack the government, spreading like the plague, shaking its foundations and system.

Ma: How was the space for the tiger work approached? Please talk about it more in-depth.

Cai: From several perspectives, one is skepticism toward heroism, and another is the sentiment of betrayal of one age against another age. The work refers in part to the folk tale of Wu Song the Tiger Slayer. At the time when Wu Song killed the tiger, it was a heroic act, but now it would be criminal. People today are skeptical of all kinds of heroes. This is a subject that shakes people's values; it is also the subject of conflict and satirical humor.

Actually, Wu Song's story was merely an excuse. The tigers being persecuted by the arrows, their struggle, distress, and pain, the physiological tension, the state of oppression and conquest, the juxtaposition of the esteem for power and empathy toward the tigers, the inappropriateness of this pain; these are my interests.

Ma: Your initial ideas for *Inopportune: Stage Two* came from images of the Egyptian pharaohs hunting lions, not tigers. And even though you talk about the story of Wu Song the Tiger Slayer, in the same breath you say that story does not have much to do with it. So why did you choose tigers?

Cai: I don't like lions very much; I like tigers. Tigers are more flesh and blood; lions are remote from contemporary society. Their power is godlike, not animal. They are too much of a cultural icon. On the other hand, tigers are more specific. Most importantly, I just like them.

Intelligent people don't listen to artists too much; they focus on the work itself. Just like a doctor doesn't pay much attention to what a patient says. Artists often think up stories for people. Some viewers mistakenly believe they have understood a work when they understand its attached story, which is only a small part. If people ask, "Why tigers?" the artist can

retort, "Why *not* tigers?" If they ask for more, I can tell the story of Wu Song, but too much of it is boring and deprives people of the opportunity to seriously consider the issues at stake. It is all too common for artworks to be too smart for their own good.

People see works like *Borrowing Your Enemy's Arrows* and hear the anecdotes behind it, but the trouble is they stop there. Why does suspending the boat and adding a Chinese story make this a work of art? Similarly, writing that I was born and educated in China and experienced Western art at such-and-such a time is easy, but the important things in between are missing. What makes what I do art? Where is the connection to history, race, the West, current society, and the art world? And, more importantly, is the work itself innovative? How has the methodology evolved? Either my work is not engaging enough, or others have not made efforts enough. At the moment Chinese exhibitions are everywhere; many people are making a living off Chinese contemporary art. But the inherent issues of presentation in these works, these in-between things, have not been properly discussed.

Ma: So why borrow the story of Wu Song at all?

Cai: The word "borrow" is correct, but the question is not *why* borrow Wu Song, but *how* – how to use tigers and arrows to command a huge exhibition hall, to direct the audience's mood, to form aesthetic perception. Simply telling the story of Wu Song and hanging up a few tigers is too simple.

I hesitated over the tigers, on whether to insert scissors, knives, and forks confiscated from an airport as I did in Sao Paolo. This would have been concrete, current, colorful. In the end I used arrows, because it was more abstract. The polemic of heroism surpasses contemporary discussions; it need not be too close to terrorism.

Ma: One thing worries me. You said you use the story of Wu Song for narrative form. Chinese artists seem to have a hard time abandoning storytelling.

Cai: Chinese artists do not need to abandon narrative. It is the scholarship of their work that must abandon its blind attention to storytelling. When an artwork uses a Chinese story, it should be critiqued in the same way that a work with gay themes is, for example. The discussions of gay-themed works are concerned with the art form engendered from homosexuality – its content, materials, color, tone, and structure – rather than useless discussion about the actual situation of being gay.

I always take from my own history, which is quite conservative. I exploit a few resources continually. One is my hometown of Quanzhou, from junk boats to Chinese medicine, from feng-shui to lanterns. My hometown is my warehouse. Another is my previous experience in stage design. My installations convey a great deal of theatricality, concepts of time, collaboration, and audience participation, as well as teamwork. The direct adaptation of theater into installation is an unexplored territory. The direct use of a stage prop in the tiger installation is an excessively palpable reaction against the installation itself, to give it some trouble. Simply having tigers writhing in mid-air with a thousand arrows in them would command

people's respect for their strength, but this would be too simplistic and safe. Interposing background scenery makes it riskier, strange, or volatile. It's best to disrupt the work. Hanging my father's painting was the same idea.

I am always looking for an imperfect thing. My oil paintings are very imperfect, so I really want to paint them, but have not spent enough time on them. I still haven't found the perfect feeling. I know I could paint more meaningful paintings, but I need to create disturbance.

Ma: You included a small oil painting in the MASS MoCA installation; it seems like an outlier. You say you are not really a painter – you make performances, installations, organize large-scale events – it is far from painting. What is it about painting that appeals to you?

Cai: The equation is very complex. When I was a child, I thought that an artist was a painter. Also, in art history those who have enlisted my passions are

Cai Guo-Qiang, *Borrowing Your Enemy's Arrows,* 1998
Museum of Modern Art, New York.
Wooden boat, straw, bamboo, arrows, flags, fan. 33 ft. long
Collection of Museum of Modern Art, New York

all painters. I am fondest of El Greco. The light, the clouds, and the churches in his paintings are illusions within his fabulous emotional world. But, contemporary society made an artist, who wanted to paint, take the path of explosion projects. Grand-scale events involve a large numbers of partners and require the mastery of all kinds of conditions and collaborations from nature to government agencies. Large-scale projects are social and revolutionary in nature, and they are hot-blooded sport events. But, I still yearn to make art that can be done at home as an amateur, not a professional, privately and sensuously, like paintings and drawings.

Ma: It is making love to the materials.

Cai: Kevin Tsai (a TV personality in Taiwan) said my drawings are my bed sheets. Luckily my drawings have done well. I can sell to collectors and sustain a certain capital for my team to do some crazy things; when funding is insufficient I can invest myself. This allows me some capital for revolutions.

Ma: An artist like you claiming to be an amateur will surprise people. You could be called one of the most professional artists around. You have a company under your name, you rely on the company for your living, people work for you, you have many clients for your works, and your exhibition schedule is arranged several years in advance. We can say that you could not be more professional. Of course, you may say that this is an abstract attitude. You often depict yourself as reckless. How do you maintain this attitude?

Cai: I must maintain this kind of amateur spirit, but an artist's team and management must be professional. Nonetheless, it is a fact that I am not very professional. I use gunpowder but have never studied it and have no license. I make car installations but can't drive – I saw large holes in the car and had to ask to find out that they were where oil tanks and engines used to be. If I were able to make realistic tigers, I would not be able to do the tiger installation, because making one tiger would have exhausted me. Non-professionalism means I don't become overly absorbed and precise toward a material. Just like the wind, when it blows across, it moves things gently. I still use gunpowder often because I screw up often. A few hundred thousand dollars worth of large outdoor projects annihilated; it makes people's blood boil. The positive side is that I am still taking risks; the negative side is that I failed. When I've played it through and through, I will stop because there will be more challenging things, like oil painting for me. Non-professionalism draws me to maintain a sense of vigor and freshness.

Ma: You take naps in the studio, which is very unprofessional! It ticks off your staff.

Cai: I'm only resting, not sleeping. As I said, the studio must be professional, even if the artist isn't.

Ma: Every time you are interviewed and asked the question about your experience in theater training and professional experience, you mention the grassroots, cooperative, and temporal natures of your work. Isn't this an oversimplification?

Cai: That is just how it is.

Ma: It has definitely influenced your working methods. Critics often use the words "theatrical" and "dramatic" when discussing your explosion projects and installations. The MASS MoCA exhibition directly brings theatrics into the foreground. What does "theatrical" mean exactly?

Cai: That is one question that I am unwilling to answer. It is the death of whoever defines it. People think that my works are theatrical, in the sense of being exaggerated. Because theater has distance between audience and stage, it is shaping a quintessence, it particularizes the effect of the scene, and I use that. Theater has undulations of high and low rhythms, processes of time, and also has strong symbolism, which I use. The theater group I worked for was a traditional opera troupe. Chinese classical aesthetics are particular about symbolism. For example, when a man and a woman look at each other, it can be symbolized by a thread connecting the eyes of the two people; a table can symbolize a mountain or home.

Ma: Minimalism was criticized for its theatricality. Critics wrote that art should be an experience of the eye and brain, rather than an immersive physical sensation. But this participatory experience has become something that contemporary art pursues.

Cai: In theater, we didn't talk much about interaction, but more about theatrical effects. But if there is no response from the audience, the theater has lost its subject. When the awareness came that the viewer is not merely a spectator but also an actor, then interaction began. Since the '90s artists have also stressed an interactive nature of their work, such as the audience participating in my installations, in a hot bath (*Cultural Melting Bath*, 1997), golf course (*Red Golf*, 1997), roller coaster (*Arbitrary History: Roller Coaster*, 2001), and yak boat (*Arbitrary History: River*, 2001). The premise of the work is that the viewer has become a performer.

I am keen to interact with people. Even though it's not my norm to go drinking with people and make friends, I communicate with others through my works. Some people do it in bed, some on boats, and some on the internet. My relationship with people occurs through my works. The more concentrated the work, the denser and thicker the relationship with people is.

Ma: In a book of paintings, the art critic Li Xianting once wrote of you:

> *Many Western art critics attribute Cai's success to his transformation of indigenous resources, such as fireworks, into new art forms. I would argue that, in addition to his talent, Cai's success in the West results from his particular charm, wisdom, courage, and enthusiasm, as well as his ability to respond to the world around him. Cai is a great joker, in the tradition of Duchamp. After Duchamp, works of art became less important than the artists themselves – their ideas, concepts and wisdom. Cai's importance lies exactly here: in taking Duchamp and pushing it to this place. "Strategy" is the key aspect of Cai's work. He uses elements of Western conceptual art... and connects them not only to various*

Cai Guo-Qiang, *Cultural Melting Bath*, 1997
Queens Museum of Art, NY. Collection of Fonds d'Art Contemporain and Musée Art Contemporain Lyon, France.
18 Taihu rocks, 1 hot tub with hydrotherapy jets, bath water infused with herbs, banyan tree root, transparent fabric, live birds

Cai Guo-Qiang, *Arbitrary History: Roller Coaster,* 2001
Collection of Musée Art Contemporain, Lyon, France.
On view at S.M.A.K. Ghent, Belgium.

types of Chinese traditions and resources but also
to historic events, art theory, and works of art that
were considered important when he was
growing up. His appeal lies in his ability to
grasp every kind of connection – societal, art
historical, environmental. Cai is also very good
at gamesmanship, playing with authority, money,
systems, concepts. And by playing his conceptual
games, he compels us, the viewers, to investigate the
life experience behind the art, its cultural traditions,
and art historical lineages in all their complexity.

Li Xianting ascribed your success to your use of strategy; you often discuss attitude and methodology. How do you cross over the enormous distance between the concept of art and the work itself?

Cai: My work looks for temporal and spatial chaos, to attain the boundlessness of life, and cast out the temptation of material gain. It is like becoming a monk, in a nihilist limitless universe. No matter how extraordinary an event is, it is also nothing extraordinary. No matter how transitory life is, it is also infinite. No matter how lacking in energy, there is still energy. Impossibility is still possibility. Because energy is infinite, no one is capable of using it up. Understanding this allows the self to be relaxed and free, at one with the universe.

However, when all is said and done, these are acquired aspirations, just like the practice of Qigong in its fate to pursue Qi, expressly pursuing oneness with the universe. I am still looking for a larger methodology, a proper attitude, pursuing a vast Dao behind the work. Dao is the highest methodology and order. My aspirations are insatiably large. I fluctuate back and forth between my abilities and reality. I seek something as lofty as the Qin Dynasty or Greek and Roman tradition, and at the same time I want contemporary effortlessness and fun. Like the work I've been busy preparing recently for the Kennedy Center of Performing Arts, *Chinese Tornado,* it must have satirical intensity, political sensitivity, and at the same time be engaging, humorous, and reckless. But behind all this there must be larger things – severity, grand schemes, and the soul of heroism.

Ma: This is also the conflict between the sublimity of modernism and cynicism of postmodernism.

Cai: The car explosion work relates to terrorism, the antagonistic conflict of civilized religions, car culture, pyrotechnics, history, and so on. But these can be said or not said, because it comes down to the appeal of the actual work on the site. In the flipping of the car, the allure of the work is already embodied: color, light, rhythm, aesthetic freshness. This is something I am good at. Making art and making love are very similar. Both require energy, materials, corporeality, a quest for Eastern and Western skills, and so on. But the key to making love is the doing of it. The key to making art is also the experience of it. Many artists have sufficient conceptual and critical knowledge and good materials, but few make works that are sufficiently alluring. That is why I insist on being an amateur, being reckless, being empathetic with the other side. To make art, you have to be stupid and extravagant. It's much more captivating!

Cai Guo-Qiang

Born: December 8, 1957, Quanzhou City, Fujian Province, China

Education: Department of Stage Design, Shanghai Drama Institute, 1981-1985

Residence: Tokyo, Japan, 1986-1995. New York, USA, 1995-present

Grants: The Institute for Contemporary Art: The National and International Studio Program 1995-1996, Asian Cultural Council Grant, New York Fondation Cartier pour l' art contemporain, Paris, 1993

Awards: *CalArts/Alpert Award in the Arts*, USA, 2001

The Venice Biennial International Prize—Golden Lion, 48th Venice Biennial, Italy, 1999

Oribe Awards, Gifu, Japan, 1997

Benesse Prize of Transculture Exhibition, 46th Venice Biennial, Italy, 1995

Japan Cultural Design Prize, Tokyo, Japan, 1995

Solo Exhibitions and Projects

2004   Curated *BMoCA:Bunker Museum of Contemporary Art*, Kinmen, Taiwan

Cai Guo-Qiang: Traveler, Freer & Sackler Gallery and Hirshhorn Museum and Sculpture Garden, Smithsonian Institution, Washington DC, USA

Cai Guo-Qiang: Inopportune, MASS MoCA, North Adams, USA

2003   *Man, Eagle and Eye in the Sky: Kite Project for Siwa, Egypt*, Siwa, Egypt (cat., video)

Light Cycle: Explosion Project for Central Park, New York, USA (video)

Explosion Event: Light Cycle Over Central Park, Asia Society and Museum, New York, USA (cat.)

Ye Gong Hao Long: Explosion Project for Tate Modern, Tate Modern, London, UK (video)

Cai Guo-Qiang: An Arbitrary History, S.M.A.K. Gent, Belgium.

Cai Guo-Qiang: For Your Pleasure Matrix 204, University of California Berkeley Art Museum, Berkeley, USA.

Curated *Pause: DMoCA Inaugural Exhibition with Kiki Smith*, Niigata, Japan (cat.)

2002   *Cai Guo-Qiang: Ethereal Flowers*, Galleria Civica di Arte Contemporanea Trento, Trento, Italy (cat.)

Transient Rainbow, Museum of Modern Art, New York, USA (video)

Cai Guo-Qiang's CHADO Pavilion—Homage to Tenshin Okakura, Hakone Open Air Museum, Hakone, Japan (cat.)

Cai Guo-Qiang, Shanghai Art Museum, Shanghai, China (cat.)

2001   *An Arbitrary History*, Musee d'art Contemporain Lyon, Lyon, France (cat.)

Artistic Direction for *APEC Cityscape Fireworks*, Asia Pacific Economic

Cooperation, Shanghai, China (video)

Curated *UMoCA* and inaugural exhibition by Ni Tsai-chin *Who Is the Happiest?*, Arte all' Arte, Arte Continua, Colla di Val d'Elsa, Italy (cat.)

Performing Chinese Ink Painting, Contemporary Art Gallery, Vancouver, Canada

Impression Oil Drawings, Charles H. Scott Gallery, Vancouver, Canada

2000 *Ascending a Staircase.* 69th Regiment Armory, New York, USA (video)

Project for Projects. Fondation Cartier pour l' art Contemporain, Paris, France (cat.)

Group Exhibitions and Projects (Selection)

2004 *Miramar Air Show*, San Diego Museum of Art, San Diego, USA

26th *Bienal Internacional Sao Paulo*, Sao Paulo, Brazil

All Under Heaven, Museum of Contemporary Art Antwerp, Antwerp, Belgium. (cat.)

The Snow Show, Rovaniemi, Finland

International Film Festival Rotterdam: Exposing Cinema, Rotterdam, The Netherlands (cat.)

2003 *Drawing Show*, University of Florida, Gainsville, Florida, USA (cat.)

The Heroic Century: The Museum of Modern Art Masterpieces, 200 Paintings and Sculptures, Museum of Fine Art, Houston, USA (cat.)

Alore, Chine? Centre Pompidou, Paris, France (cat.)

Pulse, Art, Healing, and Transformation, The Institute of Contemporary Art, Boston, USA. (cat.)

Somewhere Better Than This Place, The Contemporary Arts Center, Cincinnati, USA.

2002 *Ce Qui Arrive*, Fondation Cartier pour l'art contemporain, Paris, France. (cat.)

The First Guangzhou Triennial. Reinterpretation: A Decade of Experimental Chinese Art, Guangdong Museum of Art, Guangzhou, China

3rd *Biennale de Montréal-2002*, Montréal, Canada

The Galleries Show, The Royal Academy of Art, London, UK (video)

Magnet: Foreign Artists in Tuscany, Luigi Pecci Center for Contemporary Art, Pistoia, Italy

Tokachi International Contemporary Art Exhibition: Demeter, Obihiro, Japan (cat.)

The Power of Art—The 2nd Inaugural Show of the Prefectural Museum of Art, The Prefectural Museum of Art, Hyogo, Kobe, Japan

Red Continent, Gwangju Art Museum, Gwangju, Korea (cat.)

ev+ a 2002, Limerick City Gallery of Art, Limerick, Ireland

M Meeting, Zhejiang Library, Hangzhou, China

Art That Heals, Apexart Gallery, New York, USA

Necessity of Relationship, Galleria Civica di Arte Contemporanea, Trento, Italy (cat.)

Painting without Painting, Museum für bildende Künste, Leipzig, Germany (cat.)

2001   *Form Follows Fiction*, Castello di Rivoli Museo d'Arte Contemporanea, Turin, Italy (cat.)

Mega Wave, Yokohama 2001 International Triennale of Contemporary Art, Yokohama, Japan (cat.)

Valencia de Bienale, Valencia, Spain (cat.)

Project Refreshing, 49th Venice Biennale, Venice, Italy (cat.)

Locus/Focus, Sonsbeek 9, Arnhem, The Netherlands (cat.)

Gift, Palazzo Papesse, Siena, Italy. Scottsdale Museum of Contemporary Art, Arizona, USA (2002). The Bronx Museum of the Arts, Bronx, USA (2002) (cat.)

Visual environment for */Asunder*, Yin Mei Dance, Danspace, St. Mark's Church, New York, USA (video)

2000   *Shanghai Spirit*, Shanghai Biennial, Shanghai Museum of Art, China (cat.)

Open End—MoMA 2000, Museum of Modern Art, New York, USA (cat.)

media_city_seoul, Seoul Metropolitan Museum, Seoul, ''

Echigo-Tasumari Art Triennial, Niigata, Japan (cat.)

The Quite in the Land, Museu de Arte Moderna da Bahia, Salvador, Brazil (cat.)

Sharing Exoticism, 5th Lyon Biennale of Contemporary Art, Lyon, France (cat.)

Art/Unlimited/Basel/2000, Art/31/Basel, Basel, Switzerland

The Act of Resistance, Koldo Mitxelena Kulturunea, Donostia-San Sabastian, Spain

Biennale of Sydney 2000, Art Gallery of New South Wales, Sydney, Australia (cat.)

Over the Edges, SMAK, Gent, Belgium (cat.)

2000 Biennial Exhibition, Whitney Museum of American Art, New York, USA (cat.)

Outbound, Houston Contemporary Arts Museum, Houston, USA (cat.)

Wall, National Museum of History, Taiwan (cat.)

Gratitude, Taiwan Museum of Art, Taiwan